The Trumpeter Swan

The Trumpeter Swan

A White Perfection

Text and Photography
by Skylar Hansen

NORTHLAND PRESS FLAGSTAFF, ARIZONA

Special thanks to the personnel at the Red Rock Lakes National Wildlife Refuge for their assistance and hospitality during my visits there.

ISBN 0-87358-357-4 *Western Horizons* softcover
ISBN 0-87358-358-2 Hardcover
Library of Congress Catalog Card Number 84-60670
Composed and Printed in the United States of America

Library of Congress Cataloging in Publication Data
Hansen, Skylar.
The Trumpeter Swan
Bibliography: p. 74
1. Trumpeter swan.   I. Title
QL696.A52H34   1984   598.4'1   84-60670
ISBN 0-87358-358-2
ISBN 0-87358-357-4 (pbk.)

*To all those whose pulse quickens
at the sight of a majestic trumpeter swan*

Also by Skylar Hansen
ROAMING FREE: Wild Horses of the American West

Fish in the unruffled lakes
The swarming colors wear,
Swans in the winter air
A white perfection have,
And the great lion walks
Through his innocent grove
Lion, fish, and swan
Act, and are gone
Upon Time's toppling wave.

W. H. AUDEN
Fish in the Unruffled Lakes
1936

Contents

Author's Note

For as long as I can remember, I have counted myself among those who admire swans. Their beautiful plumage and stately posture never fail to draw my eye, inviting me to pause and gaze. Gliding across the still waters of a quiet and shaded pond that mirrors their graceful white images, they are the inspiration for many tranquil thoughts. It is easy to understand why these majestic birds have been immortalized in myth and folklore, literature, art, and tradition throughout human history.

Regardless of where I have lived or traveled, I seem always to have discovered a pair of swans nearby. Most often they were the semi-domesticated mute swans imported from Europe, common in zoos and parks. Once, when I was a child living with my family in Australia for a year, I was fortunate to glimpse a small flock of shy, wild black swans feeding in a shallow slough beside a remote outback river. For too long, though, I was completely unfamiliar with either of the two species native to the North American continent.

Then, several years ago, a friend and avid bird-watcher guided me to a marshy lake surrounded by damp coastal woodlands just an hour's drive from my home in Washington state. As dawn broke, I watched in rapt amazement while a steady stream of at least two hundred trumpeter swans, splitting the chill air with their vibrant calls, rose from the misty water and winged off into the brightening sky toward nearby fields and tidelands. The spectacle sent my imagination flying as well, and I knew that my heart had been captured by the magic of these magnificent creatures.

Soon afterward, I seriously undertook a career as a wildlife photographer, and in 1983, began a photographic pursuit of the wild trumpeter swan. Beginning in the still-frozen early springtime of Yellowstone National Park, Wyoming, I sought to document the full cycle of the trumpeter's year, from the nesting season through the raising of the young and then into the long, harsh months at the swans' secluded wintering grounds. During these times, I followed closely the successes and failures of four separate nesting pairs and their broods, and also investigated the major trumpeter population in the contiguous United States.

The nesting pairs I chose to observe and photograph included two in national parks, a third at a popular Idaho fishing lake, and a fourth at Red Rock Lakes National Wildlife Refuge. As chance would have it, this group was to present examples of both remarkable breeding success and the kinds of disappointing failure that are unfortunately all too common among this most southern remnant flock of trumpeter swans.

The nest at Christian Pond in Grand Teton National Park, Wyoming, was situated about one hundred yards from the nearest bank, in the midst of a bed of bulrushes. Moose frequently browse among the willows fringing this large, beaver-formed pond, which is also the primary habitat of many other waterfowl—Canada geese, widgeons, buffleheads, scaups, ruddy ducks, and coots—as well as trumpeters. Yellow-headed blackbirds, their raucous cries echoing in a wild chorus of alarm whenever a raven or hawk soars overhead, nest in large numbers in the bulrushes. Just within sight of Jackson Lake Lodge, this is a place where many trumpeter cygnets have been raised in years past.

At Yellowstone, I chose a pair nesting on the scenic Madison River, seven miles from the park's west entrance. Here the river flows slowly in a tangle of braided channels, meandering around sedge meadows where small herds of elk feed in the evenings and through stands of root-drowned trees, skeletons weathered to pale gray. A pair of ospreys nest a short distance upriver, atop the spire of one long-dead pine, snipe winnow in flight above the valley, and ruffed grouse drum in the dense forest that borders the river. The meadows are alive with voles rustling unseen down tunnels under the marsh grass; the river itself harbors muskrats and otters. Few trumpeters will nest in a river habitat, but this pair, whose nest was in a cattail patch in a tiny backwater, successfully established residence and was one of the park's best producers.

Encircled by the snow-covered peaks of the Continental Divide, Henry's Lake, Idaho, is world-famous for its trout fishing and is also the summer home of a pair of swans that managed to raise a brood of five the previous year, despite the commotion of many fishermen. The disturbance of passing boats forced them to abandon their former nesting site on a small island near the lake's outlet for a slough formed at the mouth of a little creek. They built their new nest in a semi-floating sedge bed, out of reach of boat wakes and storm waves alike.

The remaining pair, at Red Rock Lakes, were not included in my observations until after their brood had hatched; the refuge birds' wild nature prevented close observation until that time.

These four breeding pairs represent at least ten percent of the estimated only thirty-five to forty active nests in the tristate area of Montana, Idaho, and Wyoming in 1983. As this region supports about four hundred summering adult and subadult trumpeters, the low productivity of this breeding population is the subject of current research efforts by wildlife biologists.

It is hoped that the results of my year-long kinship with the trumpeter swan, presented in photographs and words on the following pages, will reveal in a full fashion the life, behavior, habitat, and sheer beauty of this particular species, as well as convey a sense of those ineffable qualities that account for the universal appeal of swans to humankind.

Introduction

The trumpeter was once a widespread and fairly common species of swan; they nested throughout the north-central region of the United States, south-central and northwestern Canada, and into the entire southern half of Alaska. Their winter range included the Mississippi River and broad sections of the Atlantic, Gulf, and Pacific coasts. A recent study suggests that the swans may in fact have wintered in at least some portion of all the lower forty-eight states. However, the arrival of European trappers in the nesting grounds and market-hunters to the south proved that swans, particularly the trumpeter, were as vulnerable to commercial exploitation as other native wildlife.

During the 1800s, those trumpeters that nested from Canada southward were nearly exterminated by the commercial plumage trade, hunting, and habitat destruction. Swanskins, used to make powder puffs, actually became a standard trade article of the Hudson's Bay Company as early as 1772, and continued to be sold at the London fur market until 1903. Trumpeter skins made up the vast bulk of the trade, for the tundra swans (formerly called the "whistling swan") spent the prime summer months on their far-north nesting grounds and remained largely out of the trappers' reach. The drastic decline in the trumpeter population is clearly reflected in Hudson's Bay Company swanskin tallies: between 1823 and 1880, some 108,000 swanskins were sold in London; the trade then plunged to a mere fifty-seven skins during the period between 1888 and 1897, fortunately coming to an end soon after.

Little more than a small but flourishing trade in captured live birds for private collectors remained, and trumpeter swan eggs commanded a higher price than those of the whooping crane by the last days of the nineteenth century. In 1912, a renowned ornithologist declared the trumpeter swan to be doomed to extinction within a few years.

In the early 1930s, however, there were two remnant trumpeter populations known to still exist; together, they totaled fewer than one hundred birds. Most of the sixty-odd birds in the United States were to be found in either Yellowstone National Park or in the wetlands surrounding Red Rock Lakes, part of the nearby Centennial Valley of southwestern Montana. This population persisted for several reasons: nesting locations were remote; Yellowstone National Park swans had been protected by law, as was all park wildlife beginning in 1894; and they were non-migratory despite the severe winter climate, thereby avoiding the danger of market-hunters' guns. The second group, which nested in the Grande Prairie area of Alberta, Canada, was so small and scattered that an exact count was unrecorded.

Those swans living outside Yellowstone National Park had been protected from hunting and capture in 1918 with the passage of the Migratory Bird Treaty Act (Canadian birds received the same protection a year earlier). Nevertheless, trumpeters at Red Rock Lakes continued to be shot in following years during waterfowl season, in direct violation of federal law. A further protective step was thus vital to ensure the fragile colony's survival.

The establishment of the 40,000-acre Red Rock Lakes National Wildlife Refuge in 1935 marked the beginning of a dramatic comeback for the trumpeter swan on this American range. Encompassing nearly 10,000 acres of shallow lakes and marshes—the largest mountain-marsh ecosystem in the country—this sanctuary preserved an ideal breeding habitat and protected the sensitive birds from human disturbance. Within twenty years, the refuge's swan population climbed to a peak of three hundred eighty birds. During the same period, Canada's trumpeters were also rebounding; a survey in 1944 counted seventy-eight swans: sixty-four adults and fourteen young birds.

The Yellowstone-Red Rock Lakes Refuge population (referred to as the "tristate" flock because its range includes portions of northwestern Wyoming, southwestern Montana, and northeastern Idaho) leveled out in the mid-1950s. The swans reached an apparent saturation point of about six hundred individuals, much to the disappointment

A group of non-breeding young adult birds [Widgeon Pond].

of naturalists. However, new discoveries of breeding grounds in southeastern Alaska increased the species' total census.

Until 1954, the Alaskan trumpeters were largely unrecognized, mistakenly assumed by ornithologists to be tundra swans. In fact, it was not until 1968 that a large-scale survey tallied nearly three thousand birds. This sudden boost in recognized numbers resulted in the swans' removal from "threatened with extinction" status. As a result, the trumpeter swan was not classified under the Endangered Species Act created five years later.

Revised Alaskan censuses totaled 4,170 birds in 1975 and then 7,696 in 1980. Much of this apparent sharp increase was the result of more accurate survey techniques, but protection and several good breeding years accounted for an actual population growth as well. Alaska now boasts of at least a dozen known trumpeter summer ranges. Unfavorable weather during recent nesting seasons is thought to have reduced their numbers by as many as a thousand since the last count, but the decline is viewed as only a temporary natural fluctuation.

Canada has also contributed a bright chapter to the story of the trumpeter swan. The total count of the Grande Prairie flock has doubled over the past decade to more than two hundred twenty-five birds, and the city of Grande Prairie adopted the trumpeter swan as its official bird. A population of nearly one hundred has been identified in the Toobally Lakes region of the extreme southeastern Yukon Territory, while at least another eighteen pairs are scattered over the southern half of the province. Small numbers of trumpeters also nest in British Columbia, while a very few summer in the Mackenzie District and Cypress Hills region of Saskatchewan.

Unfortunately, the population within the tri-state region has undergone a slow decline over the past two and one-half decades. The 1983 survey produced a combined count of just four hundred fifty-two adults and unfledged young, the lowest number since 1950. Wildlife biologists are not yet certain as to the exact cause of this substantial decline, and concern about the overall health and breeding vitality of the tristate flock is mounting.

In addition to these three widely separated trumpeter populations, relics of a flourishing past, a number of restoration flocks exist. The effort to transplant swans in order to repopulate former habitats actually began with the transfer of four cygnets from Red Rock Lakes to the National Elk Refuge at Jackson Hole, Wyoming, back in 1938 and continues today. Hundreds of eggs and live birds have been moved from Red Rock Lakes, and from the Grand Prairie flock, to sites in this country and in Canada.

Transplant results have been mixed. To date, the flock at LaCreek National Wildlife Refuge, South Dakota, has proven the most successful, ex-

Newly hatched cygnets begin basic preening behavior on their first day of life. Later, new wing feathers receive particularly thorough care [Madison River].

panding to populate wetlands outside the refuge, both in that state and in neighboring Nebraska. Other transplant colonies—Hennepin County Park, Minnesota; Turnbull Refuge, Washington; Malheur Refuge, Oregon; and Ruby Lake, Nevada—have become self-sustaining at best. Two in Canada have failed, but two more are proposed. A lack of suitable wintering grounds is the major obstacle in restoring the trumpeter swan to new or former habitats.

In total, then, the current trumpeter swan population falls somewhere between 8,000 and 9,000. Their smaller cousin, the tundra swan, is tenfold more plentiful. Although trumpeters are still relatively rare, by virtue of fortuitous natural circumstances and the dedicated efforts of a few far-sighted conservationists, their story over the past half-century has been one of recovery.

9

The Trumpeter Swan

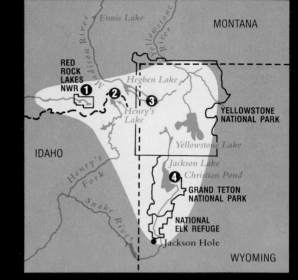

TRISTATE HABITATS

■ Trumpeter Swan Nesting Range
Studied Nest Sites
1. Red Rock Lakes
   National Wildlife Refuge
2. Henry's Lake
3. Madison River,
   Yellowstone National Park
4. Christian Pond,
   Grand Teton National Park

Modern Breeding Range

Modern Wintering Range

Historic Breeding Range

Successful Transplant Colonies

Toobally Lakes

Grande Prairie Flock

Tristate Flock

Portrait of a Swan

The trumpeter swan is the largest North American waterfowl. An adult male, called a cob, weighs from twenty-five to thirty or more pounds, while the female, or pen, averages about five pounds lighter. The plumage of both sexes is snowy white, though most birds acquire a conspicuous russet-colored stain on the feathers of the head and neck from contact with minerals and decaying vegetation in the mud of marsh and lake bottoms where they feed. The bill is black with a narrow salmon-red line along the lower mandible, and the feet are black or dark gray.

The trumpeter's appearance is quite distinctive, although in the field it is sometimes confused with the more common tundra swan. These two native swans are distinguishable at close range by the tundra's smaller size and the usually distinct yellow spot at the base of its bill. However, it is by voice that the trumpeter most clearly differs from its smaller cousin.

Sonorous and hornlike, the trumpeter's call is a sound as unforgettable as it is difficult to precisely describe. One Indian tribe aptly named the trumpeter "Ko-hoh," perhaps the best human attempt at imitation; early white explorers were similarly inspired to christen this bird in honor of its singular voice. Their calls range from a soft note indicating alertness and a sharp double-note of alarm, to bursts of staccato trumpeting and drawn-out wails. The high-pitched whistling "oo-oo-oo" cry of

Trumpeter swan, identifying salmon-red line on lower bill and typical russet stain on head feathers

RIGHT: *Trumpeter swans in flight—their wings beat with slow grace, cutting through the sky [Red Rock Lakes NWR].*

the tundra swan, which at a distance can be mistaken for that of geese, sounds weak and muffled by comparison.

Like all swans, trumpeters are graceful in water and powerful in flight—soaring on a wingspan as wide as eight feet—but rather clumsy on land. Eyesight and hearing are acute, and its wary nature makes the trumpeter difficult to approach outside of the major national parks, where the birds have become accustomed to onlookers.

Their diet consists almost exclusively of roots, tubers, stems, and leaves of freshwater aquatic plants. Pondweeds, water milfoil, waterweed, duckweed, wapato (duck potato), and white water buttercup are favored; muskgrass, sedge, tules, marestail, water moss, burreeds, spatterdocks, water lilies, and other miscellaneous vegetation are also consumed. With their long necks, which are equal to their bodies in length, trumpeters are able to gather food in the deeper shallows that are

beyond the reach of ducks and geese. They may consume up to a prodigious twenty pounds of wet vegetation daily. Also, as tundra swans have long done, trumpeters have learned to glean farm fields for waste grain in recent years.

Trumpeter swans form lifelong pair bonds, but if one of the pair dies, a new mate will likely be taken by the surviving bird before the next breeding season. Maturing birds usually become paired by their third winter, and may occupy and defend nesting territories the following spring; most trumpeters, however, do not begin breeding successfully until one to three years later. Both pen and cob share in the rearing of their brood, and young birds, or cygnets, remain with their parents until nine or ten months of age. They are then usually chased away by the parents and learn to fend for themselves.

Little is known about the typical lifespan and mortality rate of wild trumpeters, though it is assumed that few live to old age. Because of their large size and weight, swans more often fall victim to a variety of natural accidents or diseases than to attack by predators, though eagles have been seen to disable full-grown trumpeter swans in flight, and coyotes may take weak or sick birds, especially at the end of winter. Where their range overlaps with human activity or recreation areas, they often collide with power lines, ingest metal objects and lead shot while feeding, and risk being killed by indiscriminate hunters. Despite these dangers, one banded male, recovered several years ago on Idaho's Snake River, was found to have reached a record age of over twenty-five years in the wild.

Foggy morning feeding [Madison River]

The Nesting Season

*A*ccording to the calendar, spring has arrived in the high-country home of the trumpeter swan, but there is little sign that winter's firm grip on the land is weakening. A snow-mantled stillness hangs over mountain and valley, lodgepole forest and sedge meadow alike. Marshlands, bogs, creeks and rivers, shallow ponds and deep lakes not fed by warm springs are still ice-locked, their waters silent.

Yet, despite the landscape's chill expression, a palpable excitement already infects the trumpeters' wintering grounds. The birds are restless and more vocal than at any other time of the year.

Trumpeter swans occupy their nesting territories earlier than other waterfowl; at Red Rock Lakes, paired birds and small flocks may be seen visiting snow-covered marshes miles from their wintering ponds as early as February. These visits become more frequent with the passing weeks, and when the first cracks of open water appear in April, territories are permanently occupied. At Yellowstone's higher elevations, the spring thaw arrives later, delaying the appearance of nesting swans.

Experienced pairs usually reoccupy their previous year's territory. It is thus possible for the same pair to be sighted on a particular small lake or section of marsh for several consecutive years. Both birds take part in the vigorous defense of their nesting grounds, driving off either a rival mature breeding pair or their own well-grown cygnets from the

Tendrils of mist swirl among the bulrushes, rising into the chill morning air over Christian Pond in Grand Teton National Park; the incubating pen, as still as a porcelain statue, rests on the nest mound.

season before with equal vigor.

In order to raise a family, trumpeters require large territories that offer both a choice nest site and adequate feeding areas. From seventy to one hundred fifty acres of habitat are occupied by each pair at the Red Rock Lakes National Wildlife Refuge, with the largest territories located along lakeshores where open water offers a clear view of neighboring pairs. Territories established in thick marshlands are usually smaller. Mountain lakes of nine acres or more are commonly utilized in Yellowstone, and only a single pair will occupy each quiet, pine-rimmed tarn. Shallows rich in aquatic plants, quiet water free of strong currents or high waves, and a stable water level throughout spring and summer are important features of favored nesting locations.

As trumpeters become more plentiful on a given range, individual territory size does not shrink. As a result, less aggressive birds are often forced to occupy poor territories, and many young birds must delay their first nesting until a site becomes available (stable territory size is largely the reason the Red Rock Lakes trumpeter population reached a peak in the mid-1950s).

Nest building usually begins several weeks following the pair's arrival, after the chosen spot is free of snow. If last year's territory is being reestablished, then it is likely that the old nest will be repaired and used again; otherwise, a new one must be constructed. A favored spot for a nest is atop a muskrat house in areas where this water rodent is abundant; broad beds of marsh vegetation are also popular. Small islands or beaver lodges are occasionally used as nesting platforms and, more rarely, a nest can be found built directly on the shore.

The pair shares in the task of nest construction, using whatever vegetation surrounds the site—bulrushes, sedge grass, cattails—as building material. The cob, using his bill, pulls up clumps of vegetation and passes them to his mate by extending his long neck and dropping each in her direction. Meanwhile, the pen stands on top of the nest site and drags the material within her reach into a mound. Once she has shaped a suitable heap, she forms the nest cup by performing a series of settling movements. First she leans her weight forward onto her breast and paddles her webbed feet, dishing out a hollow; then she straightens to a sitting position in the hollow, rocking her body from side to side while continuing to shuffle her feet in the

hollow beneath her. Finally, she arranges and packs the nesting material tightly around her breast and flanks with a patting motion of her bill. This nest settling sequence is repeated several times, the pen orienting herself in a different direction for each repetition, until the nest cup is completed. She will continue to perform these actions during egg laying and incubation as well. Once the nest cup is established to the pen's satisfaction, she will line it with softer material, such as fine sedge grass; she may also add a small amount of down, plucked from her breast feathers, but her effort seems stingy compared with the thick down mattress that a female goose fashions to cradle her eggs.

A nest requires from a few days to two weeks to finish, and a typical mound measures six to seven feet in diameter at the base and rises to a height of nearly a foot and one-half above the water. (Nests at Red Rock Lakes were slightly smaller, while nests up to a dozen feet across have been reported in Alaska.) Young pairs, constructing a nest for the first time, are often unsuccessful because they choose poor sites, abandon their half-finished mounds, or make their nests too small to withstand minor fluctuations in water level.

On first thought, the trumpeter's method of dismantling the very cover that would otherwise act to conceal the nest seems a great disadvantage. This action, however, creates a moat of open space around the nest that will prevent the unobserved

Nest building continues through incubation, with the male gathering and shifting reeds and other plant material toward the nest and the female carefully adding each piece to the mound [Madison River].

After first clearing away the mud and loosening aquatic vegetation by churning the bottom with their powerful webs, trumpeters feed in deeper shallows by "tipping up," rather than by diving beneath the surface.

approach of predators. The size and aggressive behavior of nesting swans also makes camouflage unnecessary.

The time between arrival at the nesting territory and egg laying is critical for the trumpeter pen. During these few weeks, she feeds voraciously. Unlike the cob, who needs only to recover the strength lost during the hardships of winter, she must also accumulate sufficient energy stores to help sustain her during the long period of incubation when she alone will sit on the nest.

Egg laying usually begins in early May, with a new egg added every other day until a clutch of two to nine is completed. (In 1983, Madison River and Henry's Lake pens laid average-size clutches of five and four, respectively.) The large dull-white eggs, measuring four and one-half inches in length and weighing eleven ounces—about five times as much as a large chicken egg—soon become stained by the oil on the pen's feathers to a brownish-buff color. Sometimes the clutch of a very young or very old bird will include one or more small or malformed eggs. Weather also influences egg laying; a wet, cold spring may reduce the number of eggs a female produces and delay the process by as much as two weeks, while warm and dry weather ensures early, full-size clutches.

Alaskan trumpeters have been found to lay slightly larger eggs than the birds at Red Rock Lakes. (Interestingly, the onset of nest building, egg laying, and incubation generally coincide at these two widely separated breeding grounds. An altitude difference of over six thousand feet results in similar springtime temperatures at both latitudes.) The average clutch at the Grande Prairie grounds is five and one-half eggs, statistically over an egg larger than for the tristate flock.

Incubation begins soon after the final egg has been produced and lasts for thirty-three to thirty-seven days. During this roughly five-week period, which falls between mid-May and late-June, a pen spends all but about two hours of each day warming her clutch, while her mate remains in attendance nearby. On occasion, a male trumpeter will climb on the mound while the female is away feeding. He may rearrange nest material, or stand alert over the eggs, but never incubates them. As with most birds, this is a period of relative inactivity and simple routine, yet I was surprised to find marked differences in individual behavior among the different pairs.

The pens' feeding patterns vary widely: a typical female trumpeter leaves her nest several times for short periods during the day to forage, but the Madison River pen never fed more than twice daily. The female at Henry's Lake, however, would leave her eggs to eat as often as six times in the span of just eight hours. This could perhaps be accounted for by differences in the pens' initial fat reserves; the Madison River pen probably entered the incubation period with greater reserves and therefore required less food while on the nest.

In another behavioral variation, the Henry's Lake pen and her mate both displayed the uncommon habit of flying outside of their territory during the incubation period to forage. Usually separately, they would wing across the lake to dine in the shallows around the islet where they had nested in other years. Halfway through the incubation, the pen discontinued her trips, but the cob continued his jaunts to the island up to a few days before the hatch. He would remain at this mile-distant feeding ground for as long as an hour, and then sometimes swim leisurely back to his own territory. This behavior no doubt reflected a vestige of attachment to the old nesting site.

Feeding periods for all trumpeter pens usually last between twenty and thirty minutes. Before leaving the nest, each pen quickly covers her eggs, often pausing to pull new nesting material from the waterline onto the mound before entering the water herself. Foraging is inevitably interrupted once or twice for preening activity. Upon her return, the pen waddles heavily up a favored side of the mound, where her previous, somewhat clumsy, ascents have already formed a ramp. Standing over her eggs, she preens again for a few minutes, paying particular attention to her belly feathers. Then follows the nest-settling behavior, which she will repeat an average of six times, turning in a complete circle over the nest cup to clear away the covering she previously pulled over her eggs and reinforce the shape of the hollow. Satisfied at last, she pats nest material tightly around her body and is now prepared for another session on the clutch.

Much of the pen's nest time is spent sleeping, bill tucked securely into wing feathers; her sleep is light, however, and she is quick to raise her head, suddenly alert. Nesting trumpeter females will react even to small birds and animals near the nest. (The Christian Pond pen snapped at yellow-headed blackbirds overflying the nest, and pecked at incautious coots or muskrats that wandered up to the mound and within her reach.) The female trumpeter preens and shifts position over the clutch about twice an hour, performing the settling sequence each time. Sometimes she will also turn her eggs with her bill. Most pens appear to remain on their eggs throughout the night, though some researchers, using night scopes, have reported instances of nocturnal feeding.

I once observed the Madison River pen incubating during a heavy thundershower. She would sit almost motionless for a time, her wings slightly spread over the nest and her head tilted upward into the slanting gray downpour. Periodically shaking the water from her eyes, she would then abruptly reach back and run her bill over her limply flared wings, as if checking to see that all the feathers fit perfectly and no rainwater was penetrating to the

Madison River cob asleep on a quiet and shadowed backwater.

clutch. Then once again she would raise her head to the storm.

All three of the nests were protected from human approach by barriers of water or bottomless bog, and the females showed little or no concern when viewed from a distance. By crossing a sedge meadow and moving slowly, I was able to approach the Madison River pen to one hundred twenty-five feet and photograph her on her nest with so little disturbance that she would fall asleep immediately after my arrival. At Henry's Lake, where footing over the marshland was more treacherous, a close approach to the nest was possible only by canoe. At my first appearance on the slough, the pen slipped off the eggs when I was within two hundred feet; over the course of the next two weeks, however, she gradually allowed me to close the distance without alarming her. Eventually, I was able to anchor my craft within ninety feet of the nest and photograph her. Such an approach at Red Rock Lakes or Alaska's remote breeding grounds, where swans have little contact with humans and are easily disturbed by the presence of an observer, would have most likely resulted in an abandoned nest.

While his mate is on the eggs, the male trumpeter's chief responsibility is defending the pair's territory. In addition to attacking any other swans who have the audacity to trespass, a cob may also drive away encroaching geese, herons, cranes, white pelicans, and even surprisingly large animals. Trumpeters in the national parks and in transplant flocks, who have lost much of their natural fear of humans, have been known to drive away those approaching too near the nest with powerful blows of their wings. (The Madison River cob was always quick to position himself in the cattails between me and his incubating mate whenever he saw me approaching. Then, like the pen, he often fell asleep while I was photographing. Conversely, the male at Henry's Lake was more fearful and, perhaps intimidated by my canoe, would drift away rather than confront me.) Cobs remain more wakeful and alert than pens during the weeks of incubation. When

they do sleep, they are often close to the nest mound. The males I observed also had favored spots away from the nest. The Henry's Lake cob, in particular, preferred to sleep or loaf on a tiny grassy peninsula at the opposite end of the slough.

Like the pen, the cob continues nest-building activity until after the eggs hatch. The Madison River cob was the most industrious of the three, spending an average of several hours daily dredging up broken cattail stalks and reeds from the muddy bottom and passing them over his back toward the nest. Often, as he labored at a distance of tens of feet from his goal, he seemed to lose his bearings, passing material in the wrong direction, even further away from the nest mound. While he performed this task four or five times a day for as long as an hour at a stretch, the other two males limited their efforts to only a desultory few moments now and then.

The female may also take part in territorial defense during the incubation period, especially if the trespassers are other swans. During such defense, or whenever the pen is disturbed and departs the nest quickly, she leaves without stopping to cover her eggs, exposing them to the watchful eyes of scavengers or possible chilling if her absense is lengthy. Her participation in territorial behavior thus presents a risk to the pair's breeding success.

Exercising their territorial instincts, both the Madison River and the Christian Pond cobs seemed

The cob crouches, preparatory to launching himself at invading trumpeter swans [Madison River].

to take an almost mischievous pleasure in chasing Canada geese from their territories, especially during the geese's morning feeding period when they were particularly clamorous. Usually the swans were content just making short rushes across the water, sending their victims into hurried retreat, but at times the attacks would escalate into a fierce airborne chase, the determined male trumpeter coursing a flock of geese high above his territory.

Other birds are not the only targets of a male trumpeter swan's attention. Late one afternoon, several elk were feeding in the sedge meadow adjoining the Madison River nest when one of the sleek cows drifted near the cob's sleeping spot, a short distance from his mate. Without warning, the swan suddenly roused and launched a charge at the large animal, wings extended and trumpeting a stream of threats. The elk cow whirled, bawling in

Mate flanking mate, the Madison River pair gather themselves for a rush against rival swans invading the pair's territory.

panic, and plunged into the river to escape. The cob, flapping his wings in triumph, stood watching from the bank.

A few days later, the honking of nearby geese alerted the cob to a coyote ambling across the same meadow. This time, the trumpeter was more cautious and swam upriver to intercept the prowling coyote. Staying about twenty feet from shore, the cob watched the predator hunting voles in the marsh grass near the bank; the bird sounded low single-note calls of mild alarm until the coyote trotted back into the forest. Had the coyote shown any interest in the conspicuous nest, the male would have undoubtedly begun a threatening display, but the point at which he would have launched into an attack is uncertain.

Ironically, it was the pair that displayed the best nesting and protective behavior whose eggs appeared to be the most threatened during incubation, for their nesting site along the river was the most vulnerable to flooding. During two of the previous five years, the Madison River pen and cob had lost their clutches during the spring runoff, and the previous season's eggs had been saved only because the pair had instinctively raised the top of the nest by half a foot as the water rose. This year the river had once again risen, and for several days it seemed certain the loss would be repeated. The nest steadily disappeared and one bleak morning it looked from a distance as though the pen was sitting right on the surface of the swirling, muddy water. Fortuitously, the late spring weather turned abruptly colder, slowing the last of the high-country snow melt and reducing the river's flow. For the second year in a row, the pair's clutch escaped unscathed by high water.

As the days lengthened and moved into late June, it appeared that all of the pairs I was observing might succeed in hatching a brood of cygnets.

The trespasser turns to flee, but is overtaken and receives a firm bite to his undefended tail feathers.

Season of the Cygnets

On the morning of June 25, the Henry's Lake pen suddenly lifted herself a few inches above the clutch, letting her wings hang cupped over the hollow. At once, a little grayish-white downy figure lurched briefly in the view and then, just as quickly, disappeared.

I had decided earlier to photograph an actual hatch if an opportunity presented itself. So, ignoring sudden misgivings about disturbing the birds at such a time, I got in my canoe and paddled slowly toward the nest. The pen held her position almost until the prow nudged the mound, then stood and waddled docilely into the water to join the already-retreating cob. Arising in my unsteady craft, and looking into the hollow, I found the full hatching cycle in progress.

The oldest cygnet lay sprawled on the matting of sedge strands, its down nearly dry, but still too weak and uncoordinated to rest upright. Huddled beside the broken pieces of its egg, a second cygnet, minutes old and with its spindly seven-ounce body clothed in damp down, shook its head in a tiny spasm. A third brood member had pipped open a penny-sized hole in its egg's thick shell. The fourth and last egg had yet to show the first signs of life.

The cob and pen were eyeing me suspiciously, and I remained only long enough to shoot a dozen pictures and watch for a few moments as the oldest cygnet struggled again to find its footing and then

collapsed once more. Then, reluctantly, I left. As soon as I had back-paddled into the slough's open water, the pair returned; immediately, the pen clambered back onto the nest and covered her brood.

Upon a recheck of the nest that afternoon, I was astonished to find the adults' tempers completely transformed. Now, instead of retreating, both parents stood their ground. Wings outstretched, uttering menacing, rhythmic hisses, they confronted me with an imposing display. Standing on the rim of the mound, the pen stretched toward me, bill agape. This time, I was the one who backed away. Later, through brief, long-distance glimpses, I was able to see that the third cygnet had successfully emerged from its shell, and by nightfall, the fourth egg was completely fractured.

The following morning, soon after dawn, three of the cygnets took their first look at the world from beneath the pen's slightly outspread wings. As the

34

Hissing, wings spread to magnify the threat, the Henry's Lake pair presents a formidable warning to any intruder; though the cob is primarily responsible for defending the territory and nest, female trumpeters often become more aggressive than their mates once the cygnets hatch.

morning warmed, they scrambled about the nest and then climbed on their mother's back to bask in the bright sunlight. Had the weather been wet or chilly, the female would have continued to brood them for as long as forty-eight hours; this would not have been a hardship to the young, for they can live for several days on the remains of their yolk sacs. The fate of the fourth cygnet seemed uncertain, as the female stood and shifted position once, covering the remaining egg before resettling.

Shortly afterward, she left the nest for the first time since the hatch had begun. Ravenous, she tore and swallowed billfuls of sedge, then preened briefly before hurrying back to the brood. Within the next half-hour, she took several more breaks. On her fourth trip, the boldest cygnet attempted to follow, scrambling down the slope of the mound, but she turned and chased it back into the nest cup. Another half-hour passed before she left the nest again, and this time, the female waited with the cob for the three cygnets to join them in the water.

For a few hesitant seconds, the brood huddled at the water's edge, peeping uncertainly. Then, in turn, each of the three pushed itself afloat. With a spurt of speed, they swam forward to hug the side of the nearest adult, riding over the wavelets as lightly as puffs of thistledown. After the family swam away to feed, I once again inspected the nest and discovered the fourth cygnet curled up within the fragments of the broken shell, fully formed but dead. By and large, though, the Henry's Lake brood had a propitious beginning.

At Madison River, all five eggs hatched successfully after a full thirty-seven-day incubation period. Park rangers sighted three of the cygnets on June 20, and the remaining two the next morning. The news from Christian Pond, however, was disappointing: the nest had failed completely, every egg infertile.

Egg failure is a major cause of the low production experienced among the tristate trumpeter swan flock. Each year, from one-quarter to one-half of all eggs laid fail to hatch. The reasons for infertile clutches and high embryonic mortality are as yet unknown, although many biologists feel that the condition of the female in the early spring is an important factor. A pen still somewhat weak from the strains of winter is thought to be more likely to lay fewer and poorer eggs. A widely held theory suggests that the migratory swans of Alaska and Canada visit better feeding areas during their journey northward at winter's end, therefore producing larger clutches and bigger, healthier eggs.

Flooding accounts for most of the remaining lost eggs. In 1983 alone, one-third of the Red Rock Lakes clutches were chilled, ruined by high water that saturated nests. Predation of trumpeter eggs is rare, but skunks and ravens will occasionally raid an unattended nest, and swan pairs can offer no real

RIGHT: *During their first full day of life, settled comfortably on their mother's back, the cygnets bask in the early morning sun [Henry's Lake].*

defense against a hungry bear. Human activity at nesting sites outside the refuges will also result in abandoned nests each year.

Young cygnets dine mainly on insects, aquatic beetles, and freshwater crustaceans for the first weeks of their lives, then shift almost exclusively to a plant diet. At Henry's Lake, the hatch coincided with a sudden profusion of gnatlike flies that skimmed in dizzying patterns over the slough's surface. Within hours of entering the water, the cygnets were darting about, gobbling up as many of the bugs as they could catch; they were careful to stay within a few feet of their watchful parents, however.

Cygnets utter faint, breathy peeps as they swim and feed. When tired from paddling against waves or a sluggish current, their calls become loud and plaintive. During the second and third days of the Henry's Lake cygnets' lives, the pen continued to brood them on the nest in between feedings, while the cob rested on the mound beside her. As the cygnets grew stronger, the cob and pen became more wary of approach. Where before they had been undisturbed by my appearance in the slough, now the pair led their young from the nest—bobbing their heads and sounding the alarm—as soon as I paddled into sight.

A swan family with cygnets feeds and rests frequently throughout the day and wanders about their territory in a tightly bunched group. Both parents attend their offspring, but unlike some swan species, adult trumpeters have only rarely been sighted carrying their young on their back in the water. The young hunt in their parents' wake at first, pecking at the morsels rising to the surface as the adults feed and stir the bottom with a vigorous pumping action of their broad webs. Later, the cygnets can wrest water plants from the bottom of the shallows for themselves. When the family rests, they come ashore at favored loafing places, patches of matted-down grass at the water's edge which are easily spotted. For up to a month after hatching, the nest is used to protect the young at night and during storms; when finally abandoned, it is an untidy heap, thickly fouled with droppings.

Often, just after a feeding period and as their parents are leading them ashore, trumpeter cygnets are overcome by excitement and dive frenziedly. On occasion, an entire brood will be submerged at the same moment, with some cygnets reappearing at the same spot where they ducked under and others swimming for some distance underwater. Dashing and diving, sometimes somersaulting, their behavior seems to combine play with the benefit of bathing.

Once on land, they immediately begin to preen their down. The oil gland at the base of the swan's tail does not function in young birds, but their preening action restores the static electric charge in their down that acts to waterproof the feathers.

Henry's Lake family at three days; the female, in the lead,
can be distinguished from the male during breeding season by
her slightly uplifted tail and loosely folded wings.

Two-week old brood with pen in close attendance [Madison River]

Cygnets may display aggression toward each other at a very young age, in attempts to determine rank within their brood. An instance of this rank-order fighting occurred among the Madison River cygnets when they were only ten days old. Upon leaving the river to settle at a loafing place, two of the young birds suddenly drew themselves up to their full heights, locked bills, and scuffled for the better part of a minute before the contest ended; then, they slumped down with the rest of their broodmates to sleep. The parents made no move to interfere in the battle. Such face-to-face fighting was not observed as the birds grew older, though.

Faced with danger, cygnets will attempt to escape either by diving or hiding in marshland cover. Repeated escape dives will become shallower because the youngsters tire quickly. Finally, strength exhausted, a cygnet will manage to thrust only its head beneath the surface while paddling furiously. Young trumpeters are unable to race

Parent swans observe with interest but stand passively by as their cygnets fight to establish their rank within the brood [Yellowstone National Park].

across the water in the manner of ducklings, who with a sudden burst of speed can make a quick escape.

Throughout the observation period, I watched for signs of incipient weakness in the cygnets I was following. Trumpeter cygnets suffer a high mortality rate, especially during their first weeks. In past years, for example, forty-five to ninety percent of all young have been lost prior to fledge age at Red Rock Lakes. In the tristate region, some hatch with foot deformities that doom them to an early death. At other times, entire broods simply lose vigor and perish for unexplained reasons. Many dead cygnets are also found to be heavily infested with parasites. I was particularly concerned when the Henry's Lake brood disappeared at three weeks old, since up until that time, all the young birds under observation seemed to be doing well.

A local fisherman related a disquieting story, one that confirmed my suspicions that the cygnets had perished. He and his wife, accustomed to watching the family every day from the couple's lakeshore cabin, had spotted them as usual on the previous morning. All three cygnets appeared healthy. Just four hours later, however, they witnessed the forlorn sight of two adults, swimming alone. Such sudden disappearance of all brood members at once pointed to a predator, either animal or human.

In mid-July, misfortune also struck a swan family with six cygnets (the year's largest tristate brood) living on the seventy-five acre Widgeon Pond, at the refuge. I had just begun to follow their progress, after noting with interest that one of the young was a rare white cygnet. While such specimens appear to be albinos, they actually represent a separate color phase, known to ornithologists as white-phase or leucistic. White-phase cygnets were once regularly seen in Yellowstone, but since the 1930s, only one has been sighted in the park. During the first twenty-five years of the refuge's existance, none were sighted there. Because these birds are so rare, it was greatly disappointing that the white cygnet was the one lost from the Widgeon Pond brood; it disappeared at about two months, well past the usual age of mortality.

Through the process of attrition, I was now reduced to following just one complete brood, the Madison River group. Fortunately, it continued to thrive through the summer, all five cygnets growing noticeably with each passing week. As their muscular little necks grew longer, the family's feeding spots shifted to deeper water. Gluttonous eaters, the cygnets soon took on an overstuffed appearance. The youngsters' eagerness to feed often led to amusing antics.

They chased and snapped at dragonflies, mosquitoes, and other low-flying insects. They stole strings of vegetation that dangled from their par-

Madison River cygnet at one month

A rare white cygnet—a separate color phase rather than an albino—leads this large Red Rock Lakes brood; this color trait may be a survival disadvantage for a young bird.

Old enough to feed entirely on its own, an indolent cygnet nevertheless pesters its parent to paddle-stir for it; the cob responds by swimming away and ignoring the insistent youngster [Madison River].

ents' bills, and sometimes pecked at one another over choice bits of plant. And, despite being old enough to feed on its own, one lazy youngster persisted in seizing and tugging on the cob's flank feathers, pestering him to stir up food from the bottom for him. The cob could only escape by swimming out of this indolent cygnet's reach.

At one month, the cygnets began exhibiting a curious behavior: on hot afternoons, each would fold one leg comfortably at its side and paddle with the other. To swim in this fashion, they had to cant a bit on the water—like tiny, listing ships—in order to center the resting web under their bodies. This crooked posture seemed to be adopted as a form of relaxation, perhaps inspired by overfull stomachs.

It was also at this age that the cygnets began to molt their down. For the first time, they looked as though they had been conjured from the pages of Hans Christian Andersen's *The Ugly Duckling,* awkward and scruffy, their new feathers a shade of gray slightly darker than their down. Their bodies became rangier and their faces took on a more duck-like appearance. By ten weeks, however, the young were well-feathered in a subdued mouse-gray plumage tinged with a hint of buff-brown that paled on their underparts. The cygnets' wings showed a startling white when unfolded, and their feathers were looser and more easily ruffled by the wind than those of their parents. Black mottling extended over their bills now, forming a pattern as distinctive as a fingerprint on each individual, and their webs exhibited shades of dull yellowish-gray. Each bird weighed almost fifteen pounds at this age, a thirtyfold increase from its hatch weight (young trumpeters gain weight twice as quickly as mute swan cygnets). Somewhat clumsy, they often fell on their breasts in the mud as they stretched their wings while waddling ashore.

Adult trumpeters also molt during the summer, replacing their primary feathers; the longest molted wing feathers measure a full eighteen inches from quill tip to the end of the vane. The period during which the birds are actually flightless varies according to breeding status. The many nonbreeding swans at Red Rock Lakes molted more or less simultaneously during the month of July; they congregated in flocks on expanses of open water while their new flight feathers grew in. (On Widgeon Pond, the breeding pair tolerated the presence of about a dozen flightless nonbreeders.) Breeding

birds tend to molt a bit later, timing staggered by sex so that at least one of the pair is usually capable of flight throughout the time the cygnets are being raised. In the tristate region and Alberta, pens molt first, but in Alaska, the cobs may molt before their mates. Trumpeter swans remain flightless for approximately one month.

As the Madison River brood grew older, the family's foraging and rest periods became longer and less frequent. The swans ranged from a mile upstream of the nest site to over a mile and one-half downstream, where the river quickens into a long stretch of riffled water and shallow rapids. While downriver, they often roosted during the night on the same flat, grassy island that a wandering bull buffalo had dozed on earlier, during one warm spring afternoon.

Though still attentive to his family, the cob seemed to adopt a more relaxed attitude about guarding his rapidly developing offspring. He chose to rest a short distance from the female and the cygnets, and slept while the pen remained alert. He often watched drowsily from the shore while the rest of the family swam out to feed—but any hint of danger or sign of nervousness from his mate still brought him quickly to the family's aid. When the young were twelve weeks old the male first responded short-temperedly to them. As one of the cygnets reached underwater for the same stem of

waterweed that the adult was busy uprooting from the mud, he drove the youngster away with a sharp nip to the tailfeathers.

As the season of the cygnets advanced, the short summer began to wane. The September mornings were crisp with frost, and the mosquitoes died away. Among the lodgepole pines, squirrels were busy cutting down cones that landed with muffled thuds on the needle-carpeted forest floor. The Canada geese grew restless, flying up the river valley in the early morning and winging back downriver at dusk. Then, two days before the calendar registered the official first day of autumn, Yellowstone National Park and the banks of Madison River were blanketed with a five-inch snowfall. The following night, the thermometer plummeted to six degrees below zero, a frigid reminder that trumpeter swan cygnets must be capable of flight before the seasonal freeze-up closes most high-altitude waters.

Soon after the storm, a wandering family of otters passed through the Madison River territory. Even though the cygnets were three-quarters grown, and not likely to be victims of the otters' appetite, the swans were alarmed and fled toward shore. There, they clustered in a muddy shallow, with the cob and pen positioned in front to defend their brood. All seven birds watched tensely as the four otters, uttering loud, birdlike chirps, frolicked effortlessly in the current and then paused to share a freshly caught fish on the far riverbank. Though the cob had never hesitated to attack a harmless and slow-swimming muskrat when he saw it, he made no move to approach these swift, sinuous creatures.

After a few minutes, the male and his five cygnets abruptly shifted their attention and began dabbling their bills vigorously in the mud. Only the pen, her head upright, remained watchful. Either the male and offspring had simply lost interest in these potential predators, or the dabbling was a nervous reaction to the overlong presence of their enemies. When the otters at last meandered upstream and out of sight, the swan family swam back into deeper water without hesitation.

By October, the Madison River brood began their first serious attempts at flight. They had begun exercising their wings several times daily before three months; this practice took the form of flapping as they came ashore, chasing play behavior, and on increasingly frequent occasions, skimming in straight paths over the river's surface, beating their wings furiously.

Trumpeter cygnets are normally capable of flight by the end of their fourth month. Now, with the adults signaling the start of each effort by trumpeting, all seven members of the family flapped across the water together, with one parent usually in the lead and the second trailing the last of the struggling cygnets. It was during these family

Fully feathered in their immature plumage, the three-month old Madison River cygnets cluster behind their parents for protection; at this age, each cygnet can be identified by the individual pattern of mottled black on its bill.

In the excitement of bathing, with wild splashing and flapping, one youngster playfully rushes and then chases a lower-ranking brood mate; such behavior exercises the nearly fledged birds' wing muscles [Madison River].

exercises that the young first attempted to echo their parents' trumpeting call with single, weak, nasal-sounding notes of their own. Then, one raw and windy morning when the brood was one hundred nine days of age, the family skimmed out of view around a river bend and suddenly rose back into sight over the tall yellow sedge. All five cygnets had taken wing at once.

The brood's maiden airborne journey carried them some two hundred yards downstream; a strong head wind lifted one of the young birds above the rest and he sailed ten feet above the water. The cygnets held fairly steady in flight, but their landings were shaky, as they fought to coordinate their stalls and stretched their webs for the water. After this, the swans took several practice flights daily—chill predawn seemed to be their favorite time for exercising the cygnets' new-found skill—and the young birds' endurance grew. Within three days, the family was flying distances of up to a

*Almost airborne: at fifteen and one-half weeks and weighing
nearly twenty pounds, a Madison River cygnet gains speed
before lifting from the water on its first flight; young
trumpeters must be fledged by the time of freeze-up, or perish.*

half-mile and as high as forty feet above the river, calling continually, with the youngsters often strung out for hundreds of feet behind the lead bird.

Without a single egg or cygnet lost, this remarkable trumpeter pair had succeeded in raising the park's largest brood in over a decade to flight.

Shortly before the Madison River cygnets fledged, a flock of four subadult trumpeter swans glided in one rainy afternoon to land on the upper outskirts of the resident family's domain. The next morning, they were loosely joined by a pair of mature birds that had passed the summer several miles upriver. This sudden intrusion of foreign swans—along with flocks of nervous, noisy Canada geese fleeing hunters outside the park—seemed to leave the breeding pair, particularly the cob, tense and easily excited.

Such territorial encroachment is common late in the season. Those trumpeter pairs that establish nesting territories in the spring but are unsuccessful in raising a brood abandon their territories in late summer, and by autumn, all nonbreeding swans are prone to local wandering. Breeding birds, however, still defend their territories and may continue to do so until forced from their nesting grounds by ice.

During the following days, the four young adult swans behaved as if eager to associate more closely with the breeding pair. On occasion they drifted downstream, deeper into the pair's territory. When they swam into sight of the pen and cob, though, the pair approached and faced them, vocalizing and fluttering their wings in warning until the trespassers retreated to the territory's fringe. Some mornings, the intruding birds flew low over the family, and again the pair greeted each passing with a vociferous display. Once, the cob even flew alone upriver in pursuit.

Perhaps one, or even all, of these subadult trumpeters were offspring from the previous year, which also happened to have numbered four birds. They demonstrated little fear of humans, as though they had been raised in the park. (Evidence suggests that young swans may remain in the company of their broodmates well after leaving their parents.) The four continued to shadow the family as the current crop of cygnets took their first flight, and the breeding pair tolerated their proximity for a full week. Then the tension snapped.

Early one morning, the family returned from a downstream practice flight to discover the four birds swimming through the center of their territory, past the old nest. Immediately, the cob rushed them, but broke off the attack after just a few seconds, rejoining his mate in an elaborate triumph display of face-to-face trumpeting and quivering wings. The subadult group flew up the valley and out of sight. An hour later, the cob took wing and disappeared in their direction, apparently deter-

Breeding pairs lead their fledged offspring on regular practice flights to strengthen the young birds' wings and prepare them for migration [Widgeon Pond].

mined to force another confrontation. Upon his return several minutes later, he and the pen once again displayed in greeting, while the excited cygnets gathered around to watch. Later in the morning, the mature nonbreeding pair from upstream drifted into view of the family and was driven off by the cob.

Then, in the afternoon, the day's aggression climaxed in a furious territorial defense by the resident pair. Between the passage of two violent thunderstorms, the pair flew upriver to where the six intruding trumpeters—the four subadults and the nonbreeding pair—were gathered, feeding in the shallows. At the river's brink, the cob and pen paused to display before the group, and then the male directed his first rush at one of the rival birds. Four more attacks followed in quick succession, each interrupted by a triumph display. Twice, the pen joined her mate in his attacks. The rivals showed little fight. Each time, one bird was singled out and rushed, and its tail or wing bitten as it fled. The other swans stood quietly among the reeds and watched the action, and after about two minutes,

the nonbreeders began to disperse. When the last had flown off, the triumphant pair winged back to their cygnets. By dawn the next day, the six trespassing birds had shifted several miles up the river valley, far outside the breeding pair's domain.

It was quite a surprise when the next day, after their resolute territorial defense, the cob and pen and their cygnets suddenly lifted from the water and flew out of sight in the opposite direction, passing over the rapids that marked the downstream limit of their summer range. They had chosen to abandon the territory, despite their vigorous battle over it the previous evening and after the cygnets had been flying for only five days.

I saw the Madison River family on only one more occasion. Three weeks later, on the last day of October, they returned to their summer home for a single day. One of the cygnets was missing and I hoped that some accident had not befallen that young bird—perhaps it had gone astray and joined other trumpeters. At dusk, the family winged once again downriver, and vanished for the winter.

Breeding pair performing a triumph display after defending their territory and almost-adult offspring; the display concludes after a few moments of loud trumpeting and wing quivering.

Wintering

old seeps early into the air of trumpeter swan country. Scattered clumps of aspen flame to brilliant gold and yellow on surrounding hillsides, and then quickly drop their leaves in mute surrender. Dusted with the first permanent snowfall, once-barren rocky peaks are now poised like frothy waves of ice over the silent evergreen forests. Autumn passes, a shy hesitation, and winter descends in a sudden, white embrace.

Straddling the Continental Divide at altitudes approaching seven thousand feet, the tristate trumpeter wintering grounds exhibit some of the harshest weather conditions endured by any waterfowl. Yet, despite the months of frigid tempera-tures and deep snow, this range hosts both local trumpeters and virtually all of the Canadian swan population—a total of over twelve hundred birds—during the long season.

Migrants from the Grande Prairie flock begin appearing in Yellowstone in mid-October, making an eight hundred fifty mile journey down the eastern slopes of the Rocky Mountains, through Alberta and Montana. Traveling in small flocks and flying mostly at night, subadult birds and mature swans without broods are the first to arrive; pairs with cygnets follow about two weeks later. During the peak migration period in early November, as many as three hundred trumpeters congregate at favored bays and sandbars on Yellowstone Lake's

A mass take-off of wintering trumpeter swans from Red Rock Lakes: trumpeters must run along the water for a hundred feet or more, their broad black webs slapping and splashing loudly on the surface, to achieve flight speed.

north shore and along the first dozen miles of the Yellowstone River. They are undisturbed by human intrusion with the winter closure of the park.

Most of these swans, however, remain in central Yellowstone for only the first four to six weeks of their southern stay. By early December, ice accumulations on the river and lakeshore force them to move to lower, mid-winter grounds. The Canadian birds seem to prefer the Henry's Fork portion of the Snake River, within the boundaries of Idaho's Harriman State Park, a wildlife sanctuary, though the total number of wintering trumpeters there has declined in recent years. At Red Rock Lakes, the freeze-up usually occurs by the second week of November. Only two large ponds, fed by warm springs, remain open during the winter: Culver Pond and MacDonald Pond on the eastern boundary of the refuge. Supplemental feeding by refuge personnel enables two hundred or more trumpeters and numerous mallards and goldeneye ducks to

utilize this limited water space; swan pairs with cygnets are particularly attracted to the grain distributed here, which amounts to about five hundred bushels each season.

The National Elk Refuge is another major wintering location, sheltering up to seventy swans during the coldest months. The Madison River drainage also supports smaller numbers of birds. Warm springs maintain the open water so relied upon by the trumpeter swans in the tristate area.

Most Alaskan trumpeters winter in milder climes, migrating primarily to coastal British Columbia and Vancouver Island, with some flocks continuing as far south as Washington state. Seasonally, several hundred birds inhabit the Skagit Delta on Puget Sound, sixty miles north of Seattle, where temperatures only occasionally fall low enough to turn gentle winter rains to snow. Here, the trumpeters mingle freely with the more numerous tundra swans and feed in the company of

thousands of Siberian snow geese on tender green shoots in fields of winter wheat. Only a fraction of the large and widely dispersed Alaskan population has been accounted for by winter surveys.

In winter, the trumpeter swan reveals a social nature not apparent during other seasons. Gone are the rigid territorial behaviors of spring and summer, and the swans form loose flocks and coexist in relative harmony, collecting on the few open-water feeding areas available to them. Such close association stimulates extensive display and vocalizing among these expressive birds, and the atmosphere of a trumpeter wintering ground is permeated with excitement. On the crowded ponds at the Red Rock Lakes refuge, the nearly constant clamoring of the swans, punctuated by sudden momentary crescendos of louder trumpeting as clusters of individuals give voice in wild chorus, carries far across the silence of the snow.

The trumpeters are social creatures during the long winter, gathering in large, loosely formed flocks wherever ice-free water and food are available [Red Rock Lakes NWR].

Wings cupped, a pair glides silently downward toward the winter pond; however, descending trumpeters often give voice in unison, mingling their landing calls melodiously [Red Rock Lakes NWR].

Gestures and displays related to social behavior can be readily observed among the wintering birds. Head-bobbing, a quick up-and-down motion of the head and neck, is common; a sign of alarm at other times of the year, it now functions as a social greeting when pairs or families approach. Head-bobbing can also act as a preliminary to a trumpeting-quivering wings display by a single swan, by a pair, or most dramatically, by four or five birds at once. During the winter, instances of aggression are usually shortlived. One pair may briefly pursue another across the water, and then join in a triumph display, as if to demonstrate their prowess to the rest of the flock. Occasionally, there will be a group display, which will often end with the participants breaking apart and rushing at one another, pulling tail feathers. Actual fighting is rare.

Since the swans are no longer required to defend territories, the purpose of their displays and occasional disputes is not always clear. Much of the display behavior, however, is probably related to pair-bonding activity. Young, unpaired birds seek mates from among the wintering flock. Head-bobbing is also commonly performed between established, mature pairs as a gesture reinforcing their lifelong bond.

The trumpeters' winter diet varies, depending on the availability of aquatic plants in the ice-free areas. If duck potato or sago pondweed are present, the birds will excavate numerous foot-deep feeding pits in the water bottom, dislodging the tubers. (The swans' deep-water feeding stirs up scraps of plant material and when food is scarce, ducks and geese can often be observed feeding downstream of foraging swans.) The swans will also sometimes seek small fish during this season; researchers have noted that swans wintering on the Snake River sometimes caught and ate small trout. During unusually severe weather, even spring-fed foraging places may become iced-over and inaccessible, and then the swans must rely on fat reserves, built up during the summer and short autumn months, to sustain them. Temperatures that dropped to minus sixty degrees at the Red Rock Lakes refuge in January almost closed Culver Pond completely and forced as many as one hundred eighty birds to gather on the ten open acres of overcrowded Mac-Donald Pond. Weakened by hunger, swans are vulnerable to predators and more susceptible to disease. Even under these conditions, however, swans are reluctant to leave; it has been reported that trumpeters in British Columbia have starved to death during prolonged cold spells rather than abandon traditional wintering territories.

Trumpeter cygnets remain with their parents at the wintering grounds until late in the season, though family ties begin to weaken as early as December. Their hoarse, off-key calls blend with the din raised by the flock, but they are yet too young to socialize with the older subadult swans. In January,

Trumpeter families remain together until late winter and the approach of breeding season; these cygnets display the first white feathers of their adult plumage and will soon begin to fend entirely for themselves [Red Rock Lakes NWR].

a few white feathers begin to lighten their gray plumage, but mature feathering will not be complete until their first summer molt.

A pair with five cygnets, probably the Widgeon Pond brood, was the largest family at the refuge. Two others, identified by their neck bands as part of the Canadian Grande Prairie flock, had three-cygnet broods. Altogether, only about one in ten of the swans wintering at Red Rock Lakes was a young bird, reflecting the observation that fewer than half of all fledged cygnets survive their first winter.

As the cold season begins to wane at last, the swans grow increasingly restless. Families break up as the next breeding season approaches, and the young birds depart to wander in small flocks with other juvenile birds until they mature and form pairs. Migrant birds from Canada return to Yellowstone Lake before beginning their northward journey. Each day, the trumpeters that remain at Red Rock Lakes travel out to the frozen marshes to roost and wait for the thaw to begin.

Soon the first cracks will appear in the ice, and spring will free the nesting territories for new families, new life.

Belied by the heavy snow cover, spring approaches; a lone swan appears lost on Yellowstone Lake's icy expanse.

The Trumpeter's Future

Today, most naturalists agree that the future of the trumpeter swan is reasonably secure. Their nesting grounds enjoy the protection of refuge and national park boundaries, or better still, isolation. Existence of three major populations ensures that no single disaster could imperil the entire breeding stock. Efforts are continuing in an attempt to restore the trumpeter swan to more of its original range. Their outlook certainly appears assured, particularly when compared with the perilous status of such endangered North American species as the California condor and the whooping crane.

There are, however, several concerns that cannot be overlooked. The gradual decline of the tri-state flock continues, and researchers are still searching for reasons that will account for the trumpeter's falling numbers. Why is egg failure and cygnet mortality so high on this breeding range? What is the age of the breeding stock? Can nesting habitats be improved? It is hoped that answers to these and other questions may be found in the near future so that steps can be taken to reverse the downward trend. Of further concern is the expanding mute swan population near Yellowstone National Park. Some observers feel that these aggressive European imports may soon encroach on trumpeter territories, or even begin interbreeding with the native birds.

Limited winter habitats present another major

problem. With a growing number of Canadian trumpeters migrating to the tristate region, over-crowding on the few open-water areas may already be depleting the beds of water plants so necessary to the swans' nutrition. This concentration of birds also engenders the worry that a single outbreak of disease could seriously decimate both local and migrant populations. Research is just beginning that will help biologists better understand the movements and needs of the wintering swans; someday, it may be possible to disperse them to new winter habitats for their own ultimate benefit.

In a world where too many creatures have lost the battle of survival in the face of human greed and the ever expanding imperative for land, fate has been relatively kind to the trumpeter swan. With just a little help on our part, one of nature's finest works of avian art will continue to survive and flourish. May the clarion call of the trumpeter swan always resound across the marshland.

Sunrise gilds a quiet pond [Red Rock Lakes NWR].

Appendix

Summary of 1983 Trumpeter Swan Production, Tristate Flock

Twenty broods, totaling fifty-four young birds, were counted by the United States Fish and Wildlife Service aerial survey in mid–September. This compares with a high of one hundred eighty-seven cygnets produced in 1963 and a low of just twenty-two in 1980. The fifty-year average is seventy-seven cygnets fledged annually. Distribution over the tristate area was as follows:

WYOMING: *sixteen*
Of the three Yellowstone National Park nests, only the Madison River group was fully successful. One failed completely, and the second at Tern Lake fledged only a single bird. One brood of three in Grand Teton National Park, a brood of four at the National Elk Refuge, and another brood of three at a mountain lake in the Bridger-Teton National Forest were also raised.

MONTANA: *thirty-two*
Nineteen cygnets were counted on the Red Rock Lakes refuge, compared to the disastrous total of only four during 1982, the worst breeding year on record. Many of the cygnets were unusually small, but since the advent of cold weather was several weeks late this year, most seemed to reach flight stage by freeze-up. Twelve young were raised elsewhere in Centennial Valley, outside the refuge, and one in the nearby Beaverhead Forest.

IDAHO: *six*
Two broods were fledged in the Targhee Forest.

Bibliography

Banko, Winston E. *The Trumpeter Swan.* Lincoln: University of Nebraska Press, 1960.

Bellrose, Frank C. *Ducks, Geese, and Swans of North America.* Harrisburg, Pennsylvania: Stackpole Books, 1981.

Johnsgard, Paul A. *A Guide to North American Waterfowl.* Bloomington: Indiana University Press, 1979.

Mackenzie, John P. S. *Birds in Peril: A Guide to the Endangered Birds of the United States of America.* New York: Houghton Mifflin, 1977.

Scott, Peter. *The Swans.* New York: Houghton Mifflin, 1972.

Turner, Trudy. *Fogswamp: Living with Swans in the Wilderness.* Blaine, Washington: Hancock House, 1977

Van Wormer, Joe. *The World of the Swan.* New York: Lippincott, 1972.

Wilmore, Sylvia B. *Swans of the World.* New York: Taplinger, 1974.

UNPUBLISHED PAPERS

Hampton, Paul D. *The Wintering and Nesting Behavior of the Trumpeter Swan.*

Shea, Ruth E. *Ecology of Trumpeter Swans in Yellowstone National Park and Vicinity.*

GOVERNMENT DOCUMENTS

Annual Reports

Historical Statistical Studies

Pamphlets (various)

Trumpeter Swan Management Plan

United States Fish and Wildlife Service, Red Rock
    Lakes National Wildlife Refuge. *Tristate Trum-
    peter Swan Survey,* 1983. Washington, D.C.:
    GPO: 1983.

FOR YOUNG READERS
Fegely, Thomas D. *Wonders of Geese and Swans.*
    New York: Dodd-Mead, 1976.
Maswon, Edwin A. *Swans and Wild Geese.* Chicago:
    Follett, 1970.
McCoy, Joseph J. *Swans.* New York: Lothrop, Lee
    & Shepard, 1967.
White, E. B. *The Trumpet of the Swan.* New York:
    Harper & Row, 1970.

A hunter armed only with camera and film, Skylar Hansen grew up in Arizona exploring the state's mountains and deserts; this led to an interest in wild horses and his first photographic wildlife essay, *Roaming Free: Wild Horses of the American West*. Sighting trumpeter swans near his present-day home in Washington state inspired him to record the life stages of these elegant creatures, and, as in his previous work, he spent many months researching, making field observations, and photographing the birds.

Skylar's photography has appeared in wildlife calendars issued by Hallmark, Gibson, and Bo-Tree, among others, and, as a critical part of *Roaming Free,* has been widely acclaimed by reviewers.